A CHURCH IN THE HOUSE

A CHURCH
IN
THE HOUSE

A sermon concerning family religion
preached in London April 16, 1704.

☙

REV. MATTHEW HENRY

LATE MINISTER OF THE GOSPEL IN CHESTER

With the church that is in their house.—I CORINTHIANS 16:19

[CURIOSMITH]
MINNEAPOLIS

Published by Curiosmith.
Minneapolis, Minnesota.
Internet: curiosmith.com.

The text of this edition is from *The Miscellaneous Works of Matthew Henry* published by JOSEPH OGLE ROBINSON, 1830.

The "Guide to the Contents" was added to this edition by the publisher.

ISBN 9781946145079

GUIDE TO THE CONTENTS

A CHURCH
IN THE HOUSE

With the church that is in their house.—1 Cor. 16:19

Some very good interpreters (I know) understand this of a settled, stated, solemn meeting of Christians at the house of Aquila and Priscilla, for public worship; and they were glad of *houses* to meet in, where they wanted those better conveniences, which the church was afterwards, in her prosperous days, accommodated with. When they had not such places as they could wish, they thankfully made use of such as they could get.

But others think it is meant only of their own family and the strangers within their gates, among whom there was so much piety and devotion that it might well be called a church, or religious house. Thus the ancients generally understood it. Nor was it only Aquila and Priscilla whose house was thus celebrated for religion, (here and Romans 16:5) but Nymphas also had a church in his house.[1] Not but that others, to whom and from whom salutations are sent in Paul's epistles, made conscience of keeping up religion in their families; but these are mentioned probably because their families were more numerous than most of those other families were; which made their family devotions more solemn, and consequently more taken notice of.

In this sense I shall choose to take it, hence to recommend family religion to you, under the notion of a church in the house. When we see your public assemblies so well filled, so well frequented, we cannot but thank God and take courage; your diligent attendance on the ministry of the word and prayers, is your praise, and I trust, through grace, it redounds to your spiritual comfort and benefit. But my subject at this time will lead me to inquire into the state of religion in your private houses, whether it flourish or wither there? whether it be on the throne, or under foot there? Herein I desire to deal plainly and faithfully with your consciences, and I beg you will give them leave to deal so with you.

The pious and zealous endeavors both of magistrates and ministers for the reformation of manners and the suppression of vice and profaneness, are the joy and encouragement of all good people in the land, and a happy indication that God has yet mercy in store for us: *If the Lord had been pleased*

1 Colossians 4:15 and Philemon 1:2.

to kill us, he would not have showed us such things as these.[1] Now I know not any thing that will contribute more to the furtherance of this good work than the bringing of family-religion more into practice and reputation. Here the reformation must begin. Other methods may check the disease we complain of, but this, if it might universally obtain, would cure it. Salt must be cast into these springs, and then the waters would be healed.

Many a time, no doubt, you have been urged to this part of your duty; many a good sermon perhaps you have heard, and many a good book has been put into your hands with this design, to persuade you to keep up religion in your families, and to assist you therein: but I hope a further attempt to advance this good work, by one who is a hearty well-wisher to it, and to the prosperity of your souls and families, will not be thought altogether needless, and that by the grace of God it will not be wholly fruitless: at least it will serve to remind you of what you have received and heard to this purpose, that you may hold fast what is good, and repent of what is amiss.[2]

The lesson then which I would recommend to you from this text, is this: *That the families of Christians should be little churches;* or thus, *That wherever we have a house, God should have a church in it.*

1 Judges 13:23.
2 Revelation 3:3.

Unhappy contests there have been, and still are, among wise and good men about the constitution, order, and government of churches. God by his grace heal these breaches, lead us into all truth, and dispose our minds to love and peace; that while we endeavor herein to walk according to the light God has given us, we may charitably believe that others do so too; longing to be there where we shall be all of a mind.

But I am now speaking of churches concerning which there is no controversy. All agree that masters of families, who profess religion and the fear of God themselves, should, according to the talents they are intrusted with, maintain and keep up religion and the fear of God in their families, as those who must give account; and that families, as such, should contribute to the support of Christianity in a nation, whose honor and happiness it is to be a Christian nation. As nature makes families little kingdoms, (and perhaps economics were the first and most ancient politics) so grace makes families little churches; and those were the primitive churches of the Old Testament, before *men began to call upon the name of the Lord* in solemn assemblies, and *the sons of God came together to present themselves* before him.

Not that I would have these family churches set up and kept up in competition with, much less in contradiction to, public religious assemblies, which ought always to have the preference: *The Lord loves the gates of Sion more than all the dwellings of Jacob,*[1] and so must we; and must not forsake the assembling of ourselves together, under color of exhorting one another daily at home. Far be it from us to offer any thing that may countenance the invading of the office of the ministry, or laying it in common, and the usurping or superseding of the administration of the sacraments. No, but these family churches (which are but figuratively so) must be erected and maintained in subordination to those more sacred and solemn establishments.

Now, that I may the more distinctly open to you, and press upon you, this great duty of family religion, from the example of this and other texts, of a "church in the house," I shall endeavor, I. To show what this church in the house is, and when our families may be called churches. And, II. To persuade you by some motives, thus to turn your families into churches. And then, III. To address you upon the whole matter by way of application.

I. I am in the first place to tell you what that family religion is which will be as a church in the house, and wherein it consists, that you may see what it is we are persuading you to.

Churches are sacred societies, incorporated for the honor and service of God in Christ; devoted to God,

---

1 Psalm 87:2.

and employed for him: so should our families be.

1. Churches are societies devoted to God, called out of the world, taken in out of the common to be enclosures for God; he has set them apart for himself; and because he has chosen them, they also have chosen him, and set themselves apart for him. The Jewish church was separated to God for a *peculiar people,* a *kingdom of priests.*

Thus our houses must be churches; with ourselves we must give up our houses to the Lord, to be to him for a name and a people. All the interest we have, both in our relations and in our possessions, must be consecrated to God; as under the law all that the servant had was his master's for ever, after he had consented to have his ear bored to the door-post. When God effectually called Abram out of Ur of the Chaldees, his family assumed the appearance of a particular church; for in obedience to God's precept, and in dependence on God's promise, they took all the substance they had gathered, and the souls they had gotten, and put themselves and their all under a divine conduct and government.[1] His was a great family, not only numerous, but also very considerable; the father of it was the father of all them that believe; but even little families, jointly and entirely given up to God, so become churches. When all the members of the family yield themselves to God, subscribe

1 Genesis 12:5.

with their hands to be the Lord's, and surname themselves by the name of Israel—and the master of the family, with himself, gives up all his right, title, and interest in his house, and all that belongs to it, unto God, to be used for him, and disposed of by him; here is a church in the house.

Baptism was ordained for the discipline of nations,[1] that the kingdoms of the world, as such, might, by their conversion of the people to the faith of Christ, and the consecration of their powers and governments to the honor of Christ, become his kingdoms.[2] Thus by baptism households likewise are discipled, as Lydia's and the jailer's,[3] and in their family capacity are given up to him, who is in a particular manner the God of all the families of Israel.[4] Circumcision was at first a family ordinance, and in that particular, as well as others, baptism somewhat symbolizes with it. When the children of Christian parents are by baptism admitted members of the universal church, as their right to baptism is grounded upon, so their communion with the universal church is, during their infancy, maintained and kept up chiefly by, their immediate relation to these "churches in the house"; to them, therefore, they are, first, given back, and

---

1 Matthew 28:19.
2 Revelation 11:15.
3 Acts 16:15, 33.
4 Jeremiah 31:1.

in them they are deposited—under the tuition of them, to be trained up till they become capable of a place and a name in particular churches of larger figure and extent. So that baptized families, who own their baptism, and adhere to it, and in their joint and relative capacity make profession of the Christian faith, may so far be called little churches.

More than once in the Old Testament we read of the dedication of private houses. It is spoken of as a common practice. *What man is there that hath built a new house, and hath not dedicated it?*[1] that is, taken possession of it, in doing which it was usual to dedicate it to God by some solemn acts of religious worship. The 30ᵀᴴ Psalm is entitled, *A Psalm or Song at the Dedication of the House of David.* It is a good thing when a man has a house of his own, thus to convert it into a church, by dedicating it to the service and honor of God, that it may be a Bethel, a house of God, and not a Bethaven, a house of vanity and iniquity. Every good Christian who is a householder, no doubt does this habitually and virtually; having first given himself to the Lord, he freely surrenders all he has to him: but it may be of good use to do it actually and expressly, and often to repeat this act of resignation; *This stone which I have set for a pillar shall be God's house.*[2] Let all I have in my house,

1 Deuteronomy 20:5.
2 Genesis 28:22.

and all I do in it, be for the glory of God; I own him to be my great Landlord, and I hold all from and under him: to him I promise to pay the rents (the quit-rents) of daily praises and thanksgivings; and to do the services, the easy services of gospel obedience. Let *Holiness to the Lord* be written upon the house, and all the furniture of it, according to the word which God has spoken, That *every pot in Jerusalem and Judah shall be Holiness to the Lord of hosts.*[1] Let God by his providence dispose of the affairs of my family, and by his grace dispose the affections of all in my family, according to his will, to his own praise. Let me and mine be only, wholly, and for ever his.

Be persuaded (brethren) thus to dedicate your houses to God, and beg of him to come and take possession of them. If you never did it, do it tonight with all possible seriousness and sincerity. *Lift up your heads, O ye gates, and be ye lift up, ye ever-lasting doors, and the King of glory shall come in.*[2] Bring the ark of the Lord into the tent you have pitched, and oblige yourselves and all yours to attend it. Look upon your houses as temples for God, places for worship, and all your possessions as dedicated things, to be used for God's honor, and not to be alienated or profaned.

2. Churches are societies employed for God,

---

1 Zechariah 14:20, 21.
2 Psalm 24:7.

pursuant to the true intent and meaning of this dedication.

There are three things necessary to the well-being of a church, and which are most considerable in the constitution of it. Those are doctrine, worship, and discipline. Where the truths of Christ are professed and taught, the ordinances of Christ administered and observed, and due care taken to put the laws of Christ in execution among all who profess themselves his subjects, and this under the conduct and inspection of a gospel ministry; there is a church. And something answerable hereunto there must be in our families, to denominate them little churches.

Masters of families, who preside in the other affairs of the house, must go before their households in the things of God. They must be as prophets, priests and kings in their own families; and as such they must keep up family doctrine, family worship, and family discipline; then is there a church in the house, and this is the family religion that I am persuading you to.

(1.) Keep up family doctrine. It is not enough that you and yours are baptized into the Christian faith, profess to own the truth as it is in Jesus; but care must be taken and means used that you and yours be well acquainted with that truth, and that you grow in that acquaintance, to the honor of Christ and his holy religion, and the improvement of your own minds, and theirs who are under your charge. You must deal with your families *as men of knowledge,*[1] that is, as men who desire to grow in knowledge yourselves, and to communicate your knowledge for the benefit of others, which are the two good properties of those who deserve to be called *men of knowledge.*

That you may keep family doctrine,

[1.] You must read the Scriptures to your families, in a solemn manner, requiring their attendance on your reading, and their attention to it; and inquiring sometimes whether they understand what you read. I hope none of you are without Bibles in your houses, store of Bibles, every one a Bible. Thanks be to God we have them cheap and common in a language that we understand. The book of the law is not such a rarity as it was in Josiah's time. We need not bring this knowledge from afar, nor send from sea to sea, and from the river to the ends of the earth, to seek the word of God; no, the Word is nigh us. When popery reigned in our land, English Bibles were scarce things; a load of hay (it is said) was once given for one torn leaf of a Bible. But now Bibles are every one's money. You know where to buy them; or if not able to do that, perhaps in this charitable city you may know where to beg them. It is better to be without bread in your houses than without Bibles, for the words of God's mouth are

1 1 Peter 3:7.

and should be to you more than your necessary food.

But what will it avail you to have Bibles in your houses, if you do not use them? to have the great things of God's law and gospel written to you, if you count them as a *strange thing?* You look daily into your shop-books, and perhaps converse much with the news-books, and shall your Bibles be thrown by as an almanac out of date? It is not now penal to read the Scriptures in your families, as it was in the dawning of the day of reformation from popery, when there were those who were accused and prosecuted for reading in a certain great heretical book called an English Bible. The Philistines do not now stop up these wells, (as Genesis 26:18) nor do the shepherds drive away your flocks from them, (as Exodus 2:17) nor are they as a spring shut up, or a fountain sealed; but the gifts given to men have been happily employed in rolling away the stone from the mouth of these wells. You have great encouragements to read the Scripture; for notwithstanding the malicious endeavors of atheists to vilify sacred things, the knowledge of the Scripture is still in reputation with all wise and good men. You have also a variety of excellent helps to understand the Scripture, and to improve your reading of it; so that if you or yours perish for lack of this knowledge, as you certainly will if you persist in the neglect of it, you may thank yourselves, the guilt will lie wholly at your own doors.

Let me, therefore, with all earnestness press it upon you to make the solemn reading of the Scripture a part of your daily worship in your families. When you speak to God by prayer, be willing to hear him speak to you in his word, that there may be complete communion between you and God. This will add much to the solemnity of your family worship, and will make the transaction the more awful and serious, if it be done in a right manner; which will conduce much to the honor of God and your own and your family's edification. It will help to make the word of God familiar to yourselves, and your children and servants, that you may be ready and mighty in the Scriptures, and may thence be thoroughly furnished for every good word and work. It will likewise furnish you with matter and words for prayer, and so be helpful to you in other parts of the service. If some parts of Scripture seem less edifying, let those be most frequently read that are most so. David's Psalms are of daily use in devotion, and Solomon's Proverbs in conversation; it will be greatly to your advantage to be well versed in them. And I hope I need not press any Christian to the study of the New Testament, nor any Christian parents to the frequent instructing of their children in the pleasant and profitable histories of the Old Testament. When *you* only hear your children read the Bible, they are tempted to look upon it as no more than a school-book; but when *they* hear you read it to them in a solemn, religious manner, it comes, as it ought, with more authority. Those masters of families who make conscience of doing this daily, morning and evening, reckoning it part of that which the duty of every day requires, I am sure they have comfort and satisfaction in so doing, and find it contributes much to their own improvement in Christian knowledge, and the edification of those who dwell under their shadow; and the more, if those who are ministers expound, themselves, and other masters of families read some plain and profitable exposition of what is read, or of some part of it.

It is easy to add under this head, that the seasonable reading of other good books will contribute very much to family instruction. In helps of this kind we are as happy as any people under the sun, if we have but hearts to use the helps we have, as those who must give an account shortly of them among other talents which we are intrusted with.

[2.] You must also catechize your children and servants, so long as they continue in that age of life which needs this *milk*. Oblige them to learn some good catechism by heart, and to keep it in remembrance; and by familiar discourse with them help them to understand it, as they become capable. It is an excellent method of catechizing, which God himself directs us to,[1] to teach our children the things

1 Deuteronomy 6:7.

of God, by talking of them as we sit in the house and go by the way, when we lie down, and when we rise up. It is good to keep up stated times for this service, and be constant to them, as those who know how industrious the enemy is to sow tares while men sleep. If this good work be not kept going forward, it will of itself go backward. Wisdom also will direct you to manage your catechizing, as well as the other branches of family religion, so as not to make it a task and burden, but as much as may be a pleasure to those under your charge, that the blame may lie upon their own impiety, and not upon your imprudence, if they should say, *Behold what a weariness is it!*

This way of instruction by catechizing does in a special manner belong to the "church in the house"; for that is the nursery in which the trees of righteousness are reared, that afterwards are planted in the courts of our God. Public catechizing will turn to little account without family catechizing. The labor of ministers in instructing youth, and feeding the lambs of the flock, therefore proves to many labor in vain, because masters of families do not do their duty in preparing them for public instruction, and examining their improvement by it. As mothers are children's best nurses, so parents are, or should be their best teachers. Solomon's father was his tutor,[1] and he never forgot the lessons his mother taught him.[2]

1 Proverbs 4:3, 4.
2 Proverbs 31:1.

The baptism of your children, as it laid a strong and lasting obligation upon them to live in the fear of God, so it brought you under the most powerful engagements imaginable to bring them up in that fear. The child you gave up to God, to be dedicated to him, and admitted a member of Christ's visible church, was in God's name given back to you, with the same charge that Pharaoh's daughter gave to Moses' mother, *Take this child and nurse it for me;* and in nursing it for God, you nurse it for better preferment than that of being called the son of Pharaoh's daughter. It is worth observing, that he to whom God first did the honor of covenanting blessings upon his seed, was eminent for this part of family religion: *I know Abraham,* (says God) *that he will command his children and his household after him to keep the way of the Lord.*[1] Those, therefore, who would have the comfort of God's covenant with them and their seed, and would share in that blessing of Abraham which comes upon the Gentiles, must herein follow the example of faithful Abraham. The entail of the covenant of grace is forfeited and cut off, if care be not taken with it to transmit the means of grace. To what purpose are they discipled if they be not taught? Why did you give them a Christian name, if you will not give them the knowledge of Christ and Christianity? God has owned them as his children,

1 Genesis 18:19.

and born unto him,[1] and therefore he expects that they should be brought up for him; you are unjust to your God, unkind to your children, and unfaithful to your trust, if, having by baptism entered your children in Christ's school, and enlisted them under his banner, you do not make conscience of training them up in the learning of Christ's scholars, and under the discipline of his soldiers.

Consider what your children are now capable of, even in the days of their childhood. They are capable of receiving impressions now which may abide upon them while they live; they are turned as clay to the seal, and now is the time to apply to them the seal of the living God. They are capable of honoring God now, if they be well taught; and by their joining, as they can, in religious services with so much reverence and application as their age will admit, God is honored, and you in them present living sacrifices, holy and acceptable. The Hosannas even of children well taught will be the perfecting of praise, and highly pleasing to the Lord Jesus.

Consider what your children are designed for (we hope) in this world; they must be a seed to serve the Lord, which shall be accounted to him for a generation. They are to bear up the name of Christ in their day, and into their hands must be transmitted that good thing which is committed to us. They are to be praising God on earth, when we are

1 Ezekiel 16:20.

praising him in heaven. Let them then be brought up accordingly, that they may answer the end of their birth and being. They are designed for the service of their generation, and to do good in their day. Consult the public welfare then, and let nothing be wanting on your part to qualify them for usefulness, according as their place and capacity is.

Consider especially what they are designed for in another world: they are made for eternity. Every child you have has a precious and immortal soul that must be for ever either in heaven or hell, according as it is prepared in this present state; and, perhaps, it must remove to that world of spirits very shortly: and will it not be very mournful, if through your carelessness and neglect, your children should learn the ways of sin, and perish eternally in those ways? Give them warning, that, if possible, you may deliver their souls, at least, that you may deliver your own, and may not bring their curse and God's too, their blood and your own too, upon your heads.

I know that you cannot give grace to your children, nor is religious behavior the constant consequent of a religious education; *The race is not always to the swift, nor the battle to the strong:* but if you make conscience of doing your duty by keeping up family doctrine; if you teach them the good and the right way, and warn them of by-paths; if you reprove, exhort and encourage them as there is occasion; if you pray with them, and for them, and set them a good example, and at last consult their soul's welfare in the disposal of them, you have done your part, and may comfortably leave the issue and success with God.

(2.) Keep up family worship. You must not only as prophets teach your families, but as priests must go before them, in offering the spiritual sacrifices of prayer and praise. Herein likewise you must tread in the steps of faithful Abraham; (whose sons you are while thus you do dwell); you must not only like him instruct your household, but like him you must with them call on the name of the Lord, the everlasting God.[1] Wherever he pitched his tent, there he built an altar unto the Lord,[2] though he was yet in an unsettled state, but a stranger and a sojourner; though he was among jealous and envious neighbors, for the Canaanite and the Perizzite dwelled then in the land, yet, wherever Abraham had a tent God had an altar in it, and he himself served at that altar. Herein he has left us an example.

Families, as such, have many errands at the throne of grace, which furnish them with matter and occasion for family prayer every day; errands which cannot be done so well in secret, or public, but are fittest to be done by the family, in consort, and apart from other families. And it is good for those who lead in family devotions, ordinarily to

1 Genesis 21:33.
2 Genesis 12:7, 8; 14:4, 18.

dwell most upon the concerns of those who join in their family capacity, that it may be indeed a family prayer, not only offered up in and by the family, but suited to it. In this and other services we should endeavor not only to say something, but something to the purpose.

Five things especially you should have upon your heart in your family prayer, and should endeavor to bring something of each, more or less, into every prayer with your families.

[1.] You ought to make family acknowledgments of your dependence upon God and his providence, as you are a family. Our great business in all acts of religious worship, is to give unto the Lord the glory due unto his name; and this we must do in our family worship. Give honor to God as the founder of families by his ordinance, because "it was not good for man to be alone"; as the founder of your families by his providence, for he it is "who buildeth the house and setteth the solitary in families." Give honor to him as the owner and ruler of families; acknowledge that you and yours are his, under his government, and at his disposal, "as the sheep of his pasture." Especially adore him as the "God of all the families of Israel," in covenant relation to them, and having a particular concern for them above others.[1] Give honor to the great Redeemer as the head of all the churches, even those in your

1 Jeremiah 31:1.

houses; call him the Master of the family, and the great upholder and benefactor of it; for he it is in whom all the families of the earth are blessed.[1] All family blessings are owing to Christ, and come to us through his hand by his blood. Own your dependence upon God, and your obligations to Christ for all good things pertaining both to life and godliness; and make conscience of paying homage to your chief Lord, and never set up a title to any of your enjoyments in competition with his.

[2.] You ought to make family confessions of your sins against God; those sins you have contracted the guilt of in your family capacity. We read in Scripture of the *iniquity of the house*, as of Eli's.[2] Iniquity visited upon the children; sins that bring wrath upon families, and a curse that enters into the house to consume it, with the timber thereof, and the stones thereof.[3] How sad is the condition of those families who *sin together*, and never *pray together!* who, by concurring in frauds, quarrels, and excesses, by strengthening one another's hands in impiety and profaneness, fill the measure of family guilt, and never agree together to do any thing to empty it!

And even religious families, that are not polluted with gross and scandalous sins, yet have need to join

1 Genesis 12:3.
2 1 Samuel 3:13, 14.
3 Zechariah 5:4.

every day in solemn acts and expressions of repentance before God for their sins of daily infirmity. Their vain words and unprofitable conversation among themselves; their manifold defects in relative duties, provoking one another's lusts and passions, instead of provoking one another to love and to good works: these ought to be confessed and bewailed by the family together, that God may be glorified, and what has been amiss may be amended for the future. It was not only in a time of great and extraordinary repentance that families mourned apart,[1] but on the stated returns of the day of expiation the priest was particularly to make atonement for his household.[2] In many things we, all, offend God, and one another; and a penitent confession of it in prayer together, will be the most effectual way of reconciling ourselves both to God, and to one another. The best families, and those in which piety and love prevail most, yet in many things come short, and do enough every day to bring them upon their knees at night.

[3.] You ought to offer up family thanksgivings for the blessings which you, with your families, receive from God. Many are the mercies which you enjoy the sweetness and benefit of in common; which, if wanting to one, all the family would be sensible of it. Has not God made a hedge of

1 Zechariah 12:11.
2 Leviticus 16:17.

protection about you and your houses, and all that you have?[1] Has he not created a defense upon every "dwelling-place" of Mount Zion, as well as upon her assemblies?[2] The dreadful alarms of a storm, and the desolations made, as by a fire, once in an age, should make us sensible of our obligations to Divine Providence for our preservation from tempests and fire every day and every night. *It is of the Lord's mercies that we are not consumed,*[3] and buried in the ruins of our houses. When the whole family comes together safe in the morning from their respective retirements, and when they return safe at night from their respective employments, there having been no disaster, no "adversary," no evil occurrence—it is so reasonable and (as I may say) so natural, for them to join together in solemn thanksgivings to their great Protector, that I wonder how any who believe in a God, and a providence, can omit it. Have you not health in your family, sickness kept or taken from the midst of you? Does not God bring plentifully into your hands and increase your substance? Have you not your table spread, and your cup running over, and manna rained about your tents? and does not the whole family share in the comfort of all this? Shall not then the voice of thanksgiving be in those

1 Job 1:10.

2 Isaiah 4:5.

3 Lamentations 3:22.

tabernacles where the voice of rejoicing is?[1] Is the vine by the house-side fruitful and flourishing, and are the olive plants round the table green and growing? Are family relations comfortable and agreeable, not broken nor embittered, and shall not God be acknowledged herein, who makes every creature to be that to us that it is? Shall not the God of your mercies, your family mercies, be the God of your praises, your family praises, and that daily?

The benefit and honor of your being Christian families, your having in God's house, and within his walls, a place and a name better than that of sons and daughters, and the salvation this brings to your house, furnishes you with abundant matter for joint thanksgivings. *You hath he known above all the families of the earth*, and, therefore, he expects in a special manner to be owned by you. Of all houses, the house of Israel, the house of Aaron, and the house of Levi, have most reason to bless the Lord, and to say, *His mercy endureth for ever.*[2]

[4.] You ought to present your family petitions for the mercy and grace which your families stand need of. Daily bread is received by families together, and we are taught not only to pray for it every day, but to pray together for it, saying, *Our Father*, give it *us*. There are affairs and employments which the family is jointly concerned in the success of, and,

1 Psalm 118:15.
2 Psalm 118:29.

therefore, should jointly ask of God wisdom for the management of them, and prosperity therein. There are family cares to be cast upon God by prayer, family comforts to be sought for, and family crosses which they should together beg for the sanctification and removal of. Hereby your children will be more effectually possessed with a belief of, and regard to, the Divine Providence, than by all the instructions you can give them; which will look best in their eye, when thus reduced to practice by your daily acknowledging God in all your ways.

You desire that God will give wisdom and grace to your children, you *travail in birth again till you see Christ formed in them*,[1] you pray for them; it is well, but it is not enough; you must pray with them; let them hear you pray to God for a blessing upon the good instructions and counsels you give them; it may perhaps put them upon praying for themselves, and increase their esteem both of you and of the good lessons you teach them. You would have your servants diligent and faithful, and this perhaps would help to make them so. Masters do not give to their servants that which is just and equal, if they do not continue in prayer with them. They are put together.[2]

There are some temptations which families, as such, lie open to. Busy families are in temptation to

1 Galatians 4:19.
2 Colossians 4:1, 2.

worldliness, and neglect of religious duties; mixed families are in temptation to discord, and mutual jealousies; decaying families are in temptation to distrust, discontent, and indirect courses to help themselves; they should therefore not only watch, but pray together, that they be not overcome by the temptations they are exposed to.

There are family blessings which God has promised, and for which he will be sought unto, such as those on the house of Obed-edom for *the ark's sake;* or the mercy which the apostle Paul begs for the house of Onesiphorus.[1] These joint blessings must be sued out by joint prayers. There is a special blessing which God commands upon families that dwell together in unity,[2] which they must seek for by prayer, and come together to seek for it, in token of that unity which qualifies for it. Where God commands the blessing, we must beg the blessing. God by promise blesses David's house, and, therefore, David by prayer blesses it too.[3]

[5.] You ought also to make family intercessions for others also. There are families you stand related to, or which by neighborhood, friendship or acquaintance, you become interested in and concerned for; and these you should recommend in your prayers to the grace of God, and your family

1 2 Timothy 1:16.

2 Psalm 133:1, 3.

3 2 Samuel 6:20.

that are joined with you in the alliances should join you in those prayers. Evil tidings perhaps are received from relations at a distance, which are the grief of the family; God must then be sought unto by the family for succor and deliverance. Some of the branches of the family are, perhaps, in distant countries, and in dangerous circumstances, and you are solicitous about them; it will be a comfort to yourselves, as well as of advantage to them, to make mention of them daily in your family prayers. The benefit of prayer will reach far, because he who hears prayer can extend his hand of power and mercy to the utmost corners of the earth, and to them that are afar off upon the sea.

In the public peace likewise we and our families have peace; and therefore, if we forget thee, O Jerusalem, we are unworthy ever to stand in thy courts or dwell within thy walls. Our families should be witnesses for us that we pray daily for our land of our nativity, and the prosperity of all its interests; that praying every where we make supplication for the Queen, and all in authority.[1] That we bear upon our hearts the concerns of God's church abroad, especially the suffering parts of it. Thus keeping up a spiritual communion with all the families that in every place call on the name of the Lord Jesus.

In a word, let us go by this rule in our family

1 1 Timothy 2:3, 8.

devotions; whatever is the matter of our care, let it be the matter of our prayer; and let us allow no care which we cannot in faith spread before God. And whatever is the matter of our rejoicing, let it be the matter of our thanksgiving; and let us withhold our hearts from all those joys which do not dispose us for the duty of praise.

Under this head of family worship, I must not omit to recommend to you the singing of psalms in your families, as a part of daily worship, especially Sabbath worship. This is a part of religious worship, which participates both of the Word and prayer; for therein we are not only to give glory to God, but to teach and admonish one another; it is, therefore, very proper to make it a transition from the one to the other. It will warm and quicken you, refresh and comfort you; and, perhaps, if you have little children in your houses, they will sooner take notice of it than of any other part of your family devotion; and some good impressions may thereby be fastened upon them insensibly.

(3.) Keep up family discipline, that so you may have a complete church in your house, though in little. Reason teaches us that every man should bear rule in his own house.[1] And since that as well as other power is of God, it ought to be employed for God; and they who so rule must be just, ruling in his fear. Joshua looked further than the acts

1 Esther 1:22.

of religious worship when he made that pious resolution, *As for me and my house, we will serve the
Lord.*[1] For we do not serve him in sincerity and
truth, (which is the service he speaks of)[2] if we
and ours serve him only on our knees, and do not
take care to serve him in all the instances of religious behavior. Those only who have clean hands
and a pure heart are accounted the generation
of them that seek God.[3] And without this, those
who pretend to seek God daily do but mock him.[4]

The authority God has given over your children
and servants is principally designed for this end, that
you may thereby engage them for God and godliness. If you use it only to oblige them to do your
will, and so to serve your pride; and to do your business, and so to serve your worldliness; you do not
answer the great end of your being invested with
it: you must use it for God's honor, by it to engage
them, as far as you can, to do the will of God, and
mind the business of religion. Holy David not only
blessed his household, but took care to keep good
order in it, as appears by that plan of his family discipline, which we have in the 101st Psalm, a psalm
which Mr. Fox tells us that blessed martyr Bishop
Ridley often read to his family, as the rule by which

1 Joshua 24:15.
2 Joshua 24:14.
3 Psalm 24:4, 6.
4 Isaiah 58:2.

he resolved to govern it.

You are made keepers of the vineyard, be faithful to your trust, and carefully watch over those who are under your charge, knowing you must give account.

[1.] Countenance every thing that is good and praiseworthy in your children and servants. It is as much your duty to commend and encourage those in your family who do well, as to reprove and admonish those who do amiss; and if you take delight only in blaming that which is culpable, and are backward to praise that which is laudable, you give occasion to suspect something of an ill nature, not becoming a good man, much less a good Christian. It should be a trouble to us when we have a reproof to give, but a pleasure to us to say with the apostle, *Now I praise you*.[1]

Most people will be easier led than driven, and we all love to be spoken fair to: when you see any thing that is hopeful and promising in your inferiors, any thing of a towardly and tractable disposition, much more any thing of a pious affection to the things of God, you should contrive to encourage it. Smile upon them when you see them set their faces heavenwards, and take the first opportunity to let them know you observe it, and are well pleased with it, and do not despise the day of small things. This will quicken them to continue and abound in that which is good, it will encourage them against the difficulties they see in their way; and perhaps,

1 1 Corinthians 11:2.

may turn the wavering, trembling scale the right way, and effectually determine their resolutions to cleave to the Lord. When you see them forward to come to family worship, attentive to the Word, devout in prayer, industrious to get knowledge, afraid of sin, and careful to do their duty, let them have the praise of it, for you have the comfort of it, and God must have all the glory. Draw them with the cords of a man, hold them with the bands of love; so shall your rebukes, when they are necessary, be the more acceptable and effectual. The great Shepherd gathers the lambs in his arms, carries them in his bosom, and gently leads them; and so should you.

[2.] Discountenance every thing that is evil in your children and servants. Use your authority for the preventing of sin and the suppressing of every root of bitterness, lest it spring up, and trouble you, and thereby many be defiled. Frown upon every thing that brings sin into your families, and introduces ill words, or ill practices. Pride and passion, strife and contention, idleness and intemperance, lying and slandering, these are sins which you must not connive at, nor suffer to go without a rebuke. If you return to the Almighty, this among other things is required of you, that you *put away iniquity*, all iniquity, these and other the like iniquities, *far from your tabernacle*.[1] Make it appear that in the government of your families you are more jealous for God's

1 Job 22:23.

honor, than for your own authority and interest; and show yourselves more displeased at that which is an offense to God, than at that which is only an affront or damage to yourselves.

You must indeed be careful not to provoke your children to wrath, lest they be discouraged; and as to your servants, it is your duty to "forbear, or moderate, threatening": yet you must also, with holy zeal and resolution, and the meekness of wisdom, keep good order in your families, and set no wicked thing before their eyes, but witness against it. *A little leaven leaveneth the whole lump.*[1] Be afraid of having wicked servants in your houses, lest your children learn their way, and get a snare to their souls. Drive away with an angry countenance all that evil communication which corrupts good manners, that your houses may be habitations of righteousness, and sin may never find shelter in them.

II. I come now to offer some motives to persuade you thus to turn your families into little churches. And O that I could find out acceptable words, with which to reason with you, so as to prevail! *Suffer me a little, and I will show you* what is to be said *on God's behalf,* which is worth your consideration.

1. If your families be little churches, God will come to you and dwell with you in them; for he has said concerning the church, *This is my rest for*

1 Galatians 5:9.

ever, here will I dwell.[1] It is a very desirable thing to have the gracious presence of God with us in our families, that presence which is promised where two or three are gathered together in his name. This was it that David was so desirous of. *O when wilt thou come unto me!*[2] His palace, his court, would be as a prison, as a dungeon to him, if God did not come to him, and dwell with him in it; and cannot your hearts witness to this desire, you who have houses of your own, would you not have God come to you, and dwell with you in them? Invite him, then, beg his presence, court his stay. Nay, he invites himself to your houses by the offers of his favor and grace; *Behold, he stands at your door and knocks:*[3] it is the voice of your beloved, open to him and bid him welcome; meet him with your "Hosannas, blessed is he that cometh."[4] He comes peaceably, he brings a blessing with him, a blessing which he will cause to rest upon the habitations of the righteous.[5] He will command a blessing, which shall amount to no less than *life for evermore.*[6] This presence and blessing of God will make your relations comfortable, your affairs successful, your enjoyments sweet; and

1 Psalm 132:14.
2 Psalm 101:2.
3 Revelation 3:20.
4 Matthew 21:9.
5 Ezekiel 44:30.
6 Psalm 133:3.

behold, by it all things are made clean to you. This will make your family comforts double comforts, and your family crosses but half crosses; it will turn a tent into a temple, a cottage into a palace. *Beautiful for situation, the joy of the whole earth,*[1] are the houses in which God dwells.

Now the way to have God's presence with you in your houses is to furnish them for his entertainment. Thus the good Shunamite invited the prophet Elisha to the chamber she had prepared for him, by accommodating him there with a bed and a table, a stool and a candlestick.[2] Would you furnish your houses for the presence of God, it is not expected that you furnish them as his tabernacle was of old furnished, with blue, and purple, and scarlet, and fine linen, but set up and keep for him a throne and an altar, that from the altar you and yours may give glory to him, and from the throne he may give law to you and yours; and then you may be sure of his presence and blessing, and may solace yourselves from day to day in the comfort of it. God will be with you in a way of mercy while you are with him in a way of duty; *If you seek him he will be found of you.*[3] The secret of God shall be in your tabernacle, as it was on Job's,[4]

---

1 Psalm 48:2.

2 2 Kings 4:10.

3 1 Chronicles 28:9.

4 Job 29:4.

as it is with the righteous.[1]

2. If you make your houses little churches, God will make them his sanctuaries; nay, he will himself be to you as a little sanctuary.[2] The way to be safe in your houses, is to keep up religion and the fear of God in your houses; so shall you dwell on high, and *the place of your defense shall be the munition of rocks*.[3] The law looks upon a man's house as his castle, religion makes it truly so. If God's grace be the "glory in the midst" of the house, his providence will make a wall of fire round about it.[4] Satan found it to his confusion that God made a hedge about pious Job, about his house, and about all that he had on every side, so that he could not find one gap by which to break in upon him.[5] Every dwelling place of Mount Sion shall be protected as the tabernacle was in the wilderness, for God has promised to create upon it a cloud and smoke by day, and the shining of a flaming fire by night, which shall be a defense upon all the glory.[6] If we thus dwell in the house of the Lord all the days of our life, by making *our* houses *his* houses, we shall be hid in his pavilion, in the secret of his tabernacle shall he hide us.[7]

1 Psalm 25:14; Proverbs 3:32, 33.
2 Ezekiel 11:16.
3 Isaiah 33:16.
4 Zechariah 2:5.
5 Job 1:10.
6 Isaiah 4:5.
7 Psalm 27:4, 5.

Wherever we encamp, under the banner of Christ, the angels of God will encamp round about us, and pitch their tents where we pitch ours; and we little think how much we owe to the ministration of the good angels, that we and ours are preserved from the malice of evil angels, who are continually seeking to do mischief to good people. There are terrors that fly by night and by day, which they only who abide under the shadow of the Almighty can promise themselves to be safe from.[1] Would you insure your houses by the best policy of insurance, turn them into churches, and then they shall be taken under the special protection of Him who keeps Israel, and neither slumbers nor sleeps; and if any damage come to them, it shall be made up in grace and glory. The way of duty is without doubt the way of safety.

Praying families are kept from more mischiefs than they themselves are aware of. They are not sensible of the distinction which a kind Providence makes between them and others; though God is pleased sometimes to make it remarkable, as in the story which is credibly related of a certain village in the Canton of Bern in Switzerland, consisting of ninety houses, which in the year 1584, were all destroyed by an earthquake, except one house, in which the good man and his family were at that time together praying. That promise is sure to all

1 Psalm 91:1, 5.

the seed of faithful Abraham, *Fear not, I am thy shield*.[1] Wisdom herself has passed her word for it, *Whoso hearkeneth to me*, wherever he dwells, he *shall dwell safely, and shall be quiet from* all real evil itself, and from the amazing, tormenting *fear of evil*.[2] Nothing can hurt, nothing needs frighten, those whom God protects.

3. If you have not a church in your house, it is to be feared that Satan will have a seat there. If religion do not rule in your families, sin and wickedness will rule there. *I know where thou dwellest*, says Christ to the angel of the church of Pergamos, *even where Satan's seat is;*[3] that was his affliction: but there are many whose sin it is; by their irreligion and immorality they allow Satan a seat in their houses, and that seat a throne. They are very willing that the strong man armed should keep his palace there, and that his goods should be at peace; and the surest way to prevent this is by setting up a church in the house. It is commonly said, that where God has a church, the devil will have his chapel: but it may more truly be said in this case, where God has not a church, the devil will have his chapel. If the unclean spirit find the house in this sense empty, empty of good, though it be swept and garnished, he *taketh to himself seven other spirits more wicked*

1 Genesis 15:1.
2 Proverbs 1:33.
3 Revelation 2:13.

than himself, and they enter in and dwell there.[1]

Terrible stories have been told of houses haunted by the devil, and of the fear people have had of dwelling in such houses; verily those houses in which rioting and drunkenness reign, in which swearing and cursing are the language of the house, or in which the more spiritual wickednesses of pride, malice, covetousness and deceit have the ascendency, may truly be said to be haunted by the devil; and they are most uncomfortable houses for any man to live in; they are holds of foul spirits, and cages of unclean and hateful birds, even as Babylon the great will be when it is fallen.[2]

Now the way to keep sin out of the house is to keep up religion in the house, which will be the most effectual antidote against Satan's poison. When Abraham thought concerning Abimelech's house, *Surely the fear of God is not in this place*, he concluded no less but *they will slay me for my wife's sake.*[3] Where no fear of God is, no reading, no praying, no devotion, what can one expect but all that is bad? Where there is impiety there will be immorality; they who restrain prayer, cast off fear.[4] But if religious worship have its place in the house, it may be hoped that vice will not have a

1 Matthew 12:45.
2 Revelation 18:2.
3 Genesis 20:11.
4 Job 15:4.

place there. There is much of truth in that saying of good Mr. Dod, "Either praying will make a man give over sinning, or sinning will make a man give over praying." There remains some hope concerning those who are otherwise bad, as long as they keep up prayer. Though there be a struggle between Christ and Belial in your houses, and the insults of sin and Satan are daring and threatening, yet as long as religion keeps the field, and the weapons of its warfare are made use of, we may hope the enemy will lose ground.

4. A church in the house will make it very comfortable to yourselves. Nothing more agreeable to a gracious soul than constant communion with a gracious God; it is the *one thing* it desires, to *dwell in the house of the Lord;*[1] here it is as in its element, it is its rest for ever. If, therefore, our houses be houses of the Lord, we shall for that reason love home, reckoning our daily devotion the sweetest of our daily delights; and our family worship the most valuable of our family comforts. This will sanctify to us all the conveniences of our houses, and reconcile us to the inconveniences of it. What are Solomon's gardens, and orchards, and pools of water, and other delights of the sons of men,[2] in comparison with these delights of the children of God?

Family religion will help to make our family

---

1 Psalm 27:4.
2 Ecclesiastes 2:5, 6, 8.

relations comfortable to us, by promoting love, preventing quarrels, and extinguishing heats that may at any time happen. A family living in the fear of God, and joining daily in religious worship, truly enjoys itself; *Behold how good and how pleasant a thing it is for brethren* thus to *dwell together;*[1] it is not only like ointment and perfume which rejoice the heart, but like the holy ointment, the holy perfume, wherewith Aaron the saint of the Lord was consecrated; not only like the common dew to the grass, but like the dew which descends upon the mountains of Sion, the holy mountains.[2] The communion of saints in that which is the work of saints, is without doubt the most pleasant communion here on earth, and the liveliest representation and surest pledge of those everlasting joys which are the happiness of the spirits of just men made perfect, and the hopes of holy souls in this imperfect state.

Family religion will make the affairs of the family successful; and though they may not in every thing issue to our mind, yet we may by faith foresee that they will at last issue to our good. If this beauty of the Lord our God be upon us and our families, it will prosper the work of our hands unto us, yea, the work of our hands it will establish, or however, it will establish our hearts in that comfort which

1 Psalm 133:1.
2 Psalm 133:1, 2, 3.

makes every thing that occurs easy.[1]

We cannot suppose our mountain to stand so strong but that it will be moved; trouble in the flesh we must expect, and affliction in that from which we promise ourselves most comfort; and when Divine Providence makes our houses houses of mourning, then it will be comfortable to have them houses of prayer, and to have had them so before. When sickness, and sorrow, and death come into our families, (and sooner or later they will come) it is good that they should find the wheels of prayer going, and the family accustomed to seek God; for if we are to begin this good work when distress forces us to it, we shall drive heavily in it. They who pray constantly when they are well, may pray comfortably when they are sick.

5. A church in the house will be a good legacy, nay, it will be a good inheritance to be left to your children after you. Reason directs us to consult the welfare of posterity, and to lay up in store a good foundation for those who shall come after us to build upon; and we cannot do this better than by keeping up religion in our houses. A family altar will be the best entail; your children will for this rise up, and call you blessed, and it may be hoped they will be praising God for you, and praising God like you, here on earth, when you are praising him in heaven.

You will hereby leave your children the benefit

1 Psalm 90:17; 112:8.

of many prayers put up to heaven for them, which will be kept (as it were) upon the file there, to be answered to their comfort when you are silent in the dust. It is true of prayer, as we say of winter, "It never rots in the skies." The seed of Jacob know they do not seek in vain, though perhaps they have not to see their prayers answered. Some good Christians, who have made conscience of praying daily with and for their children, have been encouraged to hope that the children of so many prayers should not miscarry at last: and thus encouraged, Joseph's dying word has been the language of many a dying Christian's faith, *I die, but God will surely visit you.*[1] I have heard of a dutiful son who said he valued an interest in his pious father's prayers far more than his interest in his estate, though a considerable one.

You will likewise hereby leave your children a good example, which you may hope they will follow when they come into houses of their own. The usage and practice of families is commonly transmitted from one generation to another; bad customs are many times thus entailed. They who burnt incense to the queen of heaven, learnt it of their fathers.[2] And vain behavior was thus received by tradition.[3] And why may not good customs be in like manner handed down to posterity? Thus we

1 Genesis 50:24.
2 Jeremiah 44:17.
3 1 Peter 1:18.

should make known the ways of God to our children, that they may arise and declare them to their children,[1] and religion may become an heirloom in our families. Let our children be able to say, when they are tempted to sit loose to religion, That it was the way of their family, the good old way, in which their fathers walked, and in which they themselves were educated and trained up: and with this they may answer him who reproaches them. Let family worship, besides all its other pleas for itself, be able in your houses to plead prescription. And though to the acceptableness of the service, it is requisite that it be done from a higher and better principle than purely to keep up the custom of the family, yet better so than not at all: and the form of godliness may by the grace of God at length prove the happy vehicle of its power; and dry bones, whilst unburied, may be made to live. Thus *a good man leaves an inheritance to his children; and the generation of the upright shall be blessed.*[2]

6. A church in the house will contribute very much to the prosperity of the church of God in the nation. Family religion, if that prevail, will put a face of religion upon the land, and very much advance the beauty and peace of our English Jerusalem. This is that which I hope we are all hearty well wishers to; setting aside the consideration of parties, and

1 Psalm 78:6.
2 Proverbs 13:22.

separate interests, and burying all names of distinction in the grave of Christian charity, we earnestly desire to see true catholic Christianity, and serious godliness in the power of it, prevailing and flourishing in our land; to see knowledge filling the land, as the waters cover the sea; to see holiness and love giving law, and triumphing over sin and strife: we would see cause to call your city, *A city of righteousness, a faithful city, its walls salvation, and its gates praise.* Now all this would be effected, if family religion were generally set up and kept up.

When the wall was to be built about Jerusalem, it was presently done by this expedient, every one undertook to repair over against his own house.[1] And if ever the decayed walls of the gospel Jerusalem be built up, it must be by the same method. Every one must sweep before his own door, and then the street will be clean. If there were a church in every house, there would be such a church in our land as would make it a praise throughout the whole earth. We cannot better serve our country than by keeping up religion in our families.

Let families be well catechized, and then the public preaching of the word will be the more profitable and the more successful. For want of this, when we speak ever so plainly of the things pertaining to the kingdom of God, to the most

1 See Nehemiah 3:10, etc.

we do but speak parables. *The book* of the Lord is delivered to them who are not catechized, saying, *Read this*, and they say *We are not learned;* learned enough they are in other things, but not in the one thing needful.[1] But our work is easy with those who from their childhood have known the Holy Scriptures.

If every family were a praying family, public prayers would be the better joined in, more intelligently and more affectionately, for the more we are used to prayer, the more expert we shall be in that holy and divine art of "entering into the holiest" in that duty. And public reproofs and admonitions would be as a *nail in a sure place*, if masters of families would second them with their family discipline, and so clench those nails.

Religious families are blessings to the neighborhood they live in, at least by their prayers. A good man thus becomes a public good; and it is his ambition to be so. Though he see his children's children, he has small joy if he do not see peace upon Israel.[2] And therefore postponing all his own interests and satisfactions, he sets himself to seek the good of Jerusalem all the days of his life. Happy were we if there were many such. That which now remains, is to address myself to you upon the whole matter by way of exhortation; and I pray you let my counsel

---

1 Isaiah 29:12.
2 Psalm 128:5, 6.

be acceptable to you; and while I endeavor to give every one his portion, let your consciences assist me herein, and take to yourselves that which belongs to you.

III. The Application.

1. Let those masters of families who have hitherto lived in the neglect of family religion be persuaded now to set it up, and henceforward to make conscience of it. I know it is hard to persuade people to begin even a good work to which they have not been used to; yet, if God by his grace apply this word, who can tell but some may be wrought upon to comply with the design of it? We have no ill design in urging you to this part of your duty: we aim not at the advantage of a party, but purely at the prosperity of your families. We are sure we have reason on our side, and if you will but suffer that to rule you, we shall gain our point; and you will all go home firmly resolved, as Joshua was, that whatever others do themselves, and whatever they say of you, *You and your houses will serve the Lord.* God put it into, and keep it in, the imagination of the thought of your heart, and establish your way therein before him!

Proceed in the right method; first set up Christ upon the throne in your hearts, and then set up a church for Christ in your house. Let Christ dwell in your hearts by faith, and then let him dwell in your houses; you do not begin at the right end of your work, if you do not first give your own selves unto the Lord; God had respect first to Abel, and then to his offering. Let the fear and love of God rule in your hearts, and have a commanding sway and empire there, and then set up an altar for God in your tents; for you cannot do that acceptably till you have first consecrated yourselves as spiritual priests to God, to serve at that altar.

And when your hearts, like Lydia's, are opened to Christ, let your house, like hers, be opened to him too.[1] Let there be churches in all your houses; let those who have the stateliest, richest, and best furnished houses, reckon a church in them to be their best ornament: let those who have houses of the greatest care and business, reckon family religion their best employment; and not neglect the one thing needful while they are careful and cumbered about many things: nor let those who have close and mean habitations be discouraged; the ark of God long dwelt in curtains. Your dwelling is not so strait, but you may find room for a church in it. Church work is often chargeable, but you may do this church work cheap: you need not make silver shrines, as they did for Diana, nor lavish gold out of the bag, as idolaters did in the service of their gods,[2] no, *An altar of earth shall you make to your God,*[3]

---

1 Acts 16:14, 15.

2 Isaiah 46:6.

3 Exodus 20:24.

and he will accept it. Church work is accustomed to be slow work, but you may do this quickly. Put on resolution, and you may set up this tabernacle tonight, before tomorrow.

Would you keep up your authority in your family? You cannot do it better than by keeping up religion in your family. If ever the head of a family appears great, truly great, it is when he is going before his house in the service of God, and presiding among them in holy things. Then he shows himself worthy of double honor, when he teaches them the good knowledge of the Lord, and is their mouth to God in the name of God.

Would you have your family relations comfortable, your affairs successful, and give an evidence of your professed subjection to the gospel of Christ? Would you live in God's fear, and die in his favor, and escape that curse which is entailed upon prayerless families? Let religion in the power of it have its due place, that is the uppermost place in your houses.

Many objections your own corrupt hearts will make against erecting these churches, but they will appear frivolous and trifling to a pious mind, that is steadfastly resolved for God and godliness; you will never go on in your way to heaven, if you will be frightened by lions in the street. Whatever is the difficulty you dread, the discouragement you apprehend, in it, I am confident it is not insuperable, it is not unanswerable. But *he that observes the wind shall not sow, and he that regards the clouds shall not reap.*[1]

Be not loath to begin a new custom, if it be a good custom, especially if it be a duty, (as certainly this is) which, while you continue in the neglect of, you live in sin; for omissions are sins, and must come into judgment. It may be, that you have been convinced that you ought to worship God in your families, and that it is a good thing to do so; but you have put it off to some more convenient season. Will you now at last take occasion from this appeal to begin it? And do not defer so good a work any longer. The present season is without doubt the most convenient season. Begin this day; let this be the day of your laying the foundation of the Lord's temple in your house; and then consider, from this day and onward—as God by the prophet reasons with the people who neglected to build the temple[2] take notice—whether God do not from this day remarkably bless you in all that you have and do.

Plead not your own weakness and inability to perform family worship; make use of the helps that are provided for you; do as well as you can when you cannot do as well as you would, and God will accept of you. You willingly write what is necessary for the carrying on of your trade, though you

---

1 Ecclesiastes 11:4.
2 Haggai 2:18, 19.

cannot write so fine a hand as some others can; and will you not be as wise in the work of your Christian calling, to do your best, though it be far short of the best, rather than not do it at all? To him who has but one talent, and trades with that, more shall be given; but from him who buries it, it shall be taken away. Be at some pains to make the Scriptures familiar to you, especially David's Psalms, and then you cannot be at loss for a variety of apt expressions proper to be used in prayer, for they will be always at your right hand. *Take with you* those *words, words which the Holy Ghost teaches*, for you cannot find more acceptable words.

And now, shall I prevail with you in this matter? I am loath to leave you unresolved, or but almost persuaded; I beg of you, for God's sake, for Christ's sake, for your own precious soul's sake, and for the children's sake of your own bodies, that you will live no longer in the neglect of so great, and necessary, and comfortable a duty as this of family worship is. When we press upon you the more inward duties of faith and love, and the fear of God, it cannot be so evident whether we succeed in our errand as it may be in this. It is certain that you get no good by this sermon—but it is wholly lost upon you—if after you have heard it, or read it, you continue in the neglect of family religion; and if still you "cast off fear, and restrain prayer before God."[1] Your families will be

1 Job 15:4.

witnesses against you that this work was undone; and this sermon will be witness against you that it was not for want of being called to do it, but for want of a heart to do it when you were called. But I hope better things of you, my brethren, and things that accompany salvation, though I thus speak.

2. Let those who have kept up family worship formerly, but of late have left it off, be persuaded to revive it. This, perhaps, is the case of some of you; you remember the kindness of your youth, and the love of your espousals; time was when you sought God daily, and delighted to know his ways, as families who did righteousness, and forsook not the ordinances of your God; but now it is otherwise. The altar of the Lord is broken down and neglected, the daily sacrifice is ceased; and God has kept an account how many days it has ceased, whether you have or no.[1] Now God comes into your houses seeking fruit, but he finds none, or next to none: you are so eager in your worldly pursuits, that you have neither heart nor time for religious exercises. You began at first frequently to omit the service, and a small matter served for an excuse to put it by, and so by degrees it came to nothing.

O that those who have thus left their first love would now remember whence they are fallen, and repent, and do their first works! Inquire how this good work came to be neglected: was it not because

1 Daniel 8:13, 14.

your love to God cooled, and the love of the world prevailed? Have you not found a manifest decay in the prosperity of your souls since you neglected this good work? Has not sin gained ground in your hearts and in your houses? And though, when you dropped your family worship, you promised yourselves that you would make it up in secret worship, because you were not willing to allow yourselves time for both, yet have you not declined in that also? Are you not grown less frequent and less fervent in your closet devotions too? Where is now the blessedness you have formerly spoken of? I beseech you to lay out yourselves to retrieve it in time. Say as that penitent adulteress, *I will go and return to my first husband, for then it was better with me than now.*[1] Cleanse the sanctuary, and put away the strange god. Is money the god, or the belly the god that has gained possession of thy heart and house? Whatever it is, cast it out. Repair the altar of the Lord, and begin again the daily sacrifice and oblation. Light the lamps again and burn the incense. Rear up the tabernacle of David which is fallen down, lengthen its cords and strengthen its stakes, and resolve it shall never be neglected again as it has been. Perhaps you and your families have been manifestly under the rebukes of Providence since you left off your duty— as Jacob was, while he neglected to pay his vow; I beseech you hear at length the voice of the rod, and

1 Hosea 2:7.

of him who has appointed it, for it reminds you of your forgotten vows, saying, *Arise, go up to Bethel, and dwell there.*[1] Let the place thou dwellest in ever be a Bethel, so shall God dwell with thee there.

3. Let those who are remiss and negligent in their family worship be awakened to more zeal and constancy. Some of you perhaps have a church in your house, but it is not a flourishing church: it is like the church of Laodicea, neither cold nor hot; or like the church of Sardis, in which the things that remain are ready to die; so that it hath little more than a name to live. Something of this work of the Lord is done for fashion sake, but it is done deceitfully: you have in your flock a male, but you vow and sacrifice unto the Lord a corrupt thing; you grow "customary" in your accustomed services, and bring the torn and the blind, the lame and the sick, for sacrifice; and you offer that to your God which you would scorn to offer to your governor; and though it is but little you do for the church in your house, you think that too much, and say, *Behold what a weariness is it!* You put it off with a small and inconsiderable scantling of your day, and that the dregs and refuse of it. You can spare no time at all for it in the morning, nor any in the evening, till you are half asleep. It is thrust into a corner and almost lost in a crowd of worldly business and carnal behavior. When it is done, it is done so slightly, in so much haste, and with so little

1 Genesis 35:1.

reverence, that it makes no impression upon yourselves or your families. The Bible lies ready, but you have no time to read; your servants are otherwise employed, and you think it is no matter for calling them in; you yourselves can take up with a "word or two of prayer," or rest in a lifeless, heartless tale of words. Thus it is every day, and perhaps little better on the Lord's Day; no repetition, no catechizing, no singing of psalms, or none to any purpose.

Is it thus with any of your families? Is this the present state of the church in your house? My brethren, *these things ought not so to be so*. It is not enough that you do that which is good, but you must do it well. God and religion have in effect no place in your hearts or houses, if they have not the innermost and the uppermost place. Christ will come no whither to be an underling; he is not a guest to be set behind the door. What comfort, what benefit can you promise to yourselves from such trifling services as these; from an empty form of godliness without the power of it?

I beseech you, sirs, make a business of your family religion, and not a by-business. Let it be your pleasure and delight, and not a task and drudgery. Contrive your affairs so that the most convenient time may be allotted both morning and evening for your family worship, so that you may not be unfit for it, or disturbed and straitened in it; herein wisdom is profitable to direct. Address yourselves to it with reverence and seriousness, and a solemn pause; that those who join with you may see and say, that God is with you of a truth, and may be struck thereby into a like holy awe. You need not be long in the service, but you ought to be lively in it; not slothful in this business, because it is the business for God and your souls, but *fervent in spirit, serving the Lord.*[1]

4. Let those who have a church in their house be very careful to adorn and beautify it in their behaviors. If you pray in your families, and read the Scriptures, and sing psalms, and yet are passionate and froward with your relations, quarrelsome and contentious with your neighbors, unjust and deceitful in your dealings, intemperate and given to tippling, or allow yourselves in any other sinful way, you pull down with one hand what you build up with the other. Your prayers will be an abomination to God, and to good men too, if they be thus polluted. *Be not deceived, God is not mocked.*[2]

See that you be universal in your religion, that it may appear that you are sincere in it. Show that you believe a reality in it, by acting always under the commanding power and influence of it. Be not Christians upon your knees and Jews in your shops. While you seem saints in your devotions, prove not yourselves sinners in your behaviors. Having begun

1 Romans 12:11.
2 Galatians 6:7.

the day in the fear of God, be in that fear all the day long. Let the example you set your families be throughout good, and by it teach them not only to read and pray, for that is but half their work, but by it teach them to be meek and humble, sober and temperate, loving and peaceable, just and honest; so shall you adorn the doctrine of God our Savior; and those who will not be won by the Word, shall be won by your behavior. Your family worship is an honor to you, see to it that neither you nor yours be in any thing a disgrace to it.

5. Let those who are setting out in the world set up a church in their house at first, and not defer it. Plead not youth and bashfulness; if you have confidence enough to rule a family, I hope you have confidence enough to pray with a family. Say not, *The time is not come, the time that the Lord's house should be built*, as they did who *dwelt in their ceiled houses*, while God's house lay waste.[1] It ought to be built immediately; and the longer you put it off the more difficulty there will be in doing it, and the more danger that it will never be done.

Now you are beginning the world, (as you call it) is it not your wisdom as well as duty to begin with God? Can you begin better? Or can you expect to prosper if you do not begin thus? The fuller your heads are of care about setting up house, and setting up shop, and settling in both, the more need you

1 Haggai 1:2, 4.

have of daily prayer, that by it you may cast your care on God, and fetch in wisdom and direction from on high.

6. In all your removals be sure you take the "church in your house" along with you. Abraham often removed his tent, but wherever he pitched it, there the first thing he did was to build an altar. It is observable concerning Aquila and Priscilla, of whose pious family my text speaks,[1] that when St. Paul wrote his epistle to the Romans they were probably at Rome; for he sends salutations to them thither, and there it is said they had a church in their house.[2] But now, when he wrote his epistle to the Corinthians they were at Ephesus, for thence it should seem this epistle bore date, and here he sends salutations from them; and at Ephesus also they had a church in their house. As wherever we go ourselves we must take our religion with us; so wherever we take our families, or part of them, we must take our family religion with us; for in all places we need divine protection, and experience divine goodness. *I will therefore that men pray every where.*[3]

When you are in your city-houses, let not the business of them crowd out your family religion: nor let the diversions of your country-houses indispose your minds to these serious exercises. That care

1 1 Corinthians 16:19.
2 Romans 16:5.
3 1 Timothy 2:8.

and that pleasure are unseasonable and inordinate, which leave you not both heart and time to attend the service of the church in your house.

Let me here be an advocate also for those families whose masters are often absent from them, for their health or pleasure, especially on the Lord's Day, or long absent upon business. And let me beg these absent masters to consider, with whom they leave those few sheep in the wilderness,[1] and whether they do not leave them neglected and exposed. Perhaps there is not a just cause for your absence so much, nor can you give a good answer to that question, *What doest thou here, Elijah?*[2] But if there be a just cause, you ought to take care that the church in your house be not neglected when you are abroad, but that the work be done when you are not at home to do it.

7. Let inferior relatives help to promote religion in the families where they are. If family worship be not kept up in the houses where you live, let so much the more be done in your closets for God and your souls: if it be, yet think not that will excuse you from secret worship. All is little enough to keep up the life of religion in your hearts, and help you forward toward heaven.

Let the children of praying parents and the servants of praying masters, account it a great privilege

1 1 Samuel 17:28.
2 1 Kings 19:13.

to live in houses that have churches in them, and be careful to improve that privilege. Be you also ready to every good work; make the religious exercises of your family easy and pleasant to those who perform them, by showing yourselves forward to attend on them, and careful to attend to them; for your backwardness and carelessness will be their greatest discouragement. Let your lives also be a credit to good education, and make it appear to all with whom you converse, that you are every way the better for living in religious families.

8. Let solitary people, who are not engaged in families, have churches in their chambers, churches in their closets. When every man repaired the wall of Jerusalem over against his own house, we read of one that repaired over against his chamber.[1] Those who live alone out of the way of family worship, ought to take so much the more time for their secret worship, and, if possible, add the more solemnity to it. You have not families to read the Scriptures to, read them so much the more to yourselves. You have not children and servants to catechize, nor parents or masters to be catechized by; catechize yourselves then, that you may hold fast the form of sound words which you have received. *Exhort one another;* so we read it, (Hebrews 3:13) παρακαλειτε εαυτους—*exhort yourselves,* so it might as well be read. You are not made keepers of the vineyards,

1 Nehemiah 3:30.

and therefore the greater is your shame if your own vineyards you do not keep. When you are alone, yet you are not alone, for the Father is with you, to observe what you do, and to own and accept you, if you do well.

9. Let those who are to choose a settlement, consult the welfare of their souls in the choice. If a church in the house be so necessary, so comfortable, then be ye not unequally yoked with unbelievers, who will have no inclination for the church in the house, nor assist in the support of it, but instead of building this house, pluck it down with their hands.[1] Let apprenticeships and other services be chosen by this rule, that "that is best for us which is best for our souls"; and therefore it is our interest to go with those, and be with those, with whom God is.[2] When Lot was to choose a habitation, he was determined therein purely by secular advantages,[3] and God justly corrected his sensual choice, for he never had a quiet day in the Sodom he chose, till he was fired out of it. The Jewish writers tell of one of their devout rabbins, who being courted to dwell in a place which was otherwise well accommodated, but had no synagogue near, he utterly refused to accept the invitation, and gave that text for his reason, *The law of thy mouth is better to me than*

1 Proverbs 14:1.
2 Zechariah 8:23.
3 Genesis 13:11, 13.

thousands of gold and silver.[1]

10. Let religious families keep up friendship and fellowship with each other, and as they have opportunity assist one another in doing good. The communion of churches has always been accounted their beauty, strength and comfort, and so is the communion of these domestic churches. We find here, and in other of Paul's epistles, kind salutations sent to and from the houses that had churches in them. Religious families should greet one another, visit one another, love one another, pray for one another, and as becomes households of faith, do all the good they can one to another; forasmuch as they all meet daily at the same throne of grace, and hope to meet shortly at the same throne of glory, to be no more, as they are now, divided in Jacob, and scattered in Israel.

Lastly, Let those houses that have churches in them, flourishing churches, have comfort in them. Is religion in the power of it uppermost in your houses? And are you and yours serving the Lord, serving him daily? Go on and prosper, for the Lord is with you, while you be with him. See your houses under the protection and blessing of heaven, and be assured that all things shall work together for good to you. Make it to appear by your holy cheerfulness that you find God a good master, Wisdom's ways pleasantness, and her paths peace; and that you see

1 Psalm 119:72.

no reason to envy those who spend their days in carnal mirth, for you are acquainted with better pleasures than any they can pretend to.

Are your houses on earth God's houses? Are they dedicated to him and employed for him? Be of good comfort, his house in heaven shall be yours shortly: *In my Father's house there are many mansions;*[1] and there is one, you may be sure, for each of you, who thus *by a patient continuance in well-doing, seek for glory, honor, and immortality.*[2]

---

1 John 14:2.
2 Romans 2:7.

NOTES

MAN'S QUESTIONS & GOD'S ANSWERS

Am I accountable to God?
Each of us will give an account of himself to God. ROMANS 14:12 (NIV).

Has God seen all my ways?
Everything is uncovered and laid bare before the eyes of him to whom we must give account. HEBREWS 4:13 (NIV).

Does he charge me with sin?
But the Scripture declares that the whole world is a prisoner of sin. GALATIANS 3:22 (NIV).
All have sinned and fall short of the glory of God. ROMANS 3:23 (NIV).

Will he punish sin?
The soul who sins is the one who will die. EZEKIEL 18:4 (NIV).
For the wages of sin is death, but the gift of God is eternal life in Christ Jesus our Lord. ROMANS 6:23 (NIV).

Must I perish?
He is patient with you, not wanting anyone to perish, but everyone to come to repentance. 2 PETER 3:9 (NIV).

How can I escape?
Believe in the Lord Jesus, and you will be saved. ACTS 16:31 (NIV).

Is he able to save me?
Therefore he is able to save completely those who come to God through him. HEBREWS 7:25 (NIV).

Is he willing?
Christ Jesus came into the world to save sinners. 1 TIMOTHY 1:15 (NIV).

Am I saved on believing?
Whoever believes in the Son has eternal life, but whoever rejects the Son will not see life, for God's wrath remains on him. JOHN 3:36 (NIV).

Can I be saved now?
Now is the time of God's favor, now is the day of salvation. 2 CORINTHIANS 6:2 (NIV).

As I am?
Whoever comes to me I will never drive away. JOHN 6:37 (NIV).

Shall I not fall away?
Him who is able to keep you from falling. JUDE 1:24 (NIV).

If saved, how should I live?
Those who live should no longer live for themselves but for him who died for them and was raised again. 2 CORINTHIANS 5:15 (NIV).

What about death and eternity?
I am going there to prepare a place for you. I will come back and take you to be with me that you also may be where I am. JOHN 14:2-3 (NIV).

www.ingramcontent.com/pod-product-compliance
Lightning Source LLC
Chambersburg PA
CBHW020603030426
42337CB00013B/1194